HEALING FROM BETRAYAL

A Guide To Rebuilding Your Marriage After An Affair

By

TEDDY COLE

Table of Content

CHAPTER 1 : THE BREACH

Infidelity is described as a breach of an emotional and/or sexual exclusivity between a partnership. When individuals marry, they agree to abandon all others and commit themselves entirely to their chosen mate.

Sarah

Every day, there may be a time when I do not consider this. The agony is indescribable. This was a guy I loved but who blamed me for his infidelity. He said he didn't have a choice. That it is my fault that I am who I am. I believed I was someone who loved and was loved, but it turns out that when our kid was born, this ended. Six years ago. He brings up statements I made to him, and arguments we had years ago as if he has kept a record of all my flaws to use against me in this manner. As an explanation to justify his acts.

This was a man I had given my whole life to, the father of my kid, and I never imagined he could do anything like this. Is this to say he never appreciated what he had? Is it true that having a family means nothing to him? One of his frequent observations is "Children are adaptable. he'll grow out of it. It isn't a huge deal ".

Peter

I was crushed when I discovered my wife was having an affair, and much more so when she chose to divorce me.

What Is The Definition Of Betrayal?

An affair is a breach of trust that involves another person and violates the promise of marriage to be faithful in your affections and actions.

Pornography, neglect, abuse, and other damaging circumstances are all betrayals of trust in marriage. However, I will define infidelity as a sexual or emotional encounter or relationship between a married person and someone who is not that person's spouse.

The unfaithfulness could be romantic or sexual, involving physical contact to express romance, physical attraction, or sexual desire i.e. holding hands, hugging, kissing, intercourse, etc.

The betrayal could be emotional, resulting from an intense bond between two people that mimics the closeness and emotional intimacy of a marriage relationship.
A cyber affair with sexual or emotional undertones could take place "via chat, webcam, email, text, social media, or other forms of communication."

One of the most painful experiences a lover or spouse can have is learning that their partner is having or has had an affair. When someone feels deceived, they may experience a broad range of feelings, from profound grief to severe despair to frenzied wrath, and everything in between. There is no perfect set of emotions for this common experience. The consequences of an affair on a relationship may vary from absolute ruin to a desire to learn from the affair and seek to rebuild the relationship.

No matter how mentally tough you are, the feeling of betrayal is difficult to overcome. This is especially true in a married relationship because you invest your emotions in that person. After all, you and they exchanged a sacred vow. When your spouse violates that vow, it can be devastating, even life-changing. Some people are so traumatized that they see no reason to live again. Others have been so deeply traumatized that they are unable to forgive or trust again.

It is often simpler to abandon a relationship that has been harmed by an affair than it is to go beyond the hurt and reassess the connection. It takes a lot of guts and commitment to reestablish trust, assess one's own role in the status of their relationship and put up the effort necessary to make the relationship work. Similarly, facing one's flaws, character flaws, and anxieties requires enormous humility on the part of the unfaithful partner before moving on to gain forgiveness.

The betrayed spouse has been bombarded with so many emotions that practically any sensation is normal. An affair often leaves a person feeling violated, alone, distrusting, and full of self-doubt. A terrible sense of loss, as if the earth under one's feet had been yanked out from under them and they were hanging in space. Many losses may occur, including loss of faith, feeling of specialness, self-esteem, and sense of purpose, to mention a few.

A sensation of disorientation may overwhelm one with so much uncertainty that one experiences a loss of identity. While one may feel as if he or she is going insane, considering the depth of the trauma, these sentiments are normal. The unfaithful spouse may also be experiencing a range of emotions. However, no matter how bad he or she feels, it pales in comparison to what the betrayed partner feels. It is much less devastating for the unfaithful spouse than it is for the betrayed.

Some individuals feel that once a partner cheats, the relationship is gone. They may also assume that once trust has been betrayed, it is hard to regain it.

Whether one decides to just put the affair behind them without exploring any of the circumstances that may have contributed to the affair, one risks spending a life continuously worrying if it will happen again. All of one's queries remain unanswered; one learns nothing, and one leaves the ground ripe for it to happen again or for mistrust to grow. Neither side gets the chance to learn from the event.

If one decides to stay in the relationship and allow the affair to continue, he or she is almost ensuring a life of bitterness, guilt, rage, despair, and loss of self-respect. Unless both spouses consent to sexually open marriage and have the maturity to carry it out appropriately, the majority of situations where it has been attempted have not proved to be viable.

The last choice, staying together and attempting to restore one's relationship, allows both parties to benefit from the experience. It offers the highest chance of strengthening and progressing the connection.

Although you may feel hopeless right now, you must remember that there is hope—and a way out. While it will take willingness, repentance, and intentionality to recover from an affair, you and your spouse can do so by responding decisively and well to this unwelcome trial.

The good news is that as a marriage counselor I have discovered that couples who choose to recover from and rebuild their relationships after infidelity often end up with stronger, more loving, and mutually understanding relationships than they had before.

CHAPTER 2 : HOW TO HANDLE A CHEATING SPOUSE

Dealing with a cheating spouse may be one of the most difficult tasks you will ever face. When it comes to determining whether or not to make things work, there is no right or wrong answer. All you can do is talk to your spouse, listen to yourself, and determine if your marriage is worth preserving. If you do decide to make things work, you must take things one day at a time and remember to take care of yourself.

Sarah

Every day, there may be a time when I do not consider this. The agony is indescribable. This was a guy I loved but who blamed me for his infidelity. He said he didn't have a choice. That it is my fault that I am who I am. I believed I was someone who loved and was loved, but it turns out that when our kid was born, this ended. Six years ago. He brings up statements I made to him, and arguments we had years ago as if he has kept a record of all my flaws to use against me in this manner. As an explanation to justify his acts.

I assumed that all relationships had ups and downs. You don't blame the other person for your difficulties; you work through them. I honestly believed that the previous year had been our year of working through issues and developing our relationship. But it comes out that he has been having an affair with a lady on the other side of the globe, continuously messaging, and taking regular overseas trips under the cover of work or visiting family for the whole year. Work calls kept coming in. But why has he been paying attention to me for the last year? Why should you sleep with me? Why should you spend your vacation with me? Travel?

I've had a hunch for months that he was interacting with her. It's generally after having sex with me. He would be aloof and gloomy the following day. Then I'd look for the messages. What exactly does this mean? Does sleeping with me make him feel bad about 'cheating' on her? I can't make sense of his actions, the way he rejects everything, even though it has been going on for more than a year. "Get over it," or "Oh, we're back to that," he says, defending himself, assuring me it's not his fault, that it's just between us, recounting things he's said about our relationship and our kid. I'm at a lost, and it's clear that he has no sorrow or sentiments. The secrecy, lying, denial, and blame-shifting are just too much for me to stomach. I believe time cures all wounds. But the ache I'm experiencing will not go away.

This was a man I had given my whole life to, the father of my kid, and I never imagined he could do anything like this. Is this to say he never appreciated what he had? Is it true that having a family means nothing to him? One of his frequent observations is "Children are adaptable. he'll grow out of it. It isn't a huge deal ".

1. You Are Not To Blame

Your spouse's motivations for infidelity may not always be evident, and you may feel compelled to blame yourself. Perhaps you believe you've been aloof, or that you haven't been truthful in the bedroom. Perhaps you've let work take over and haven't made enough time for your relationship.

However, although these may be reasons that your relationship needs more effort, you should be aware that nothing you do can ever drive your spouse to cheat, and you should never blame yourself for your spouse's faults. Sure, you could be to blame for a particular issue in the relationship, and it's crucial to admit that.

You should never, ever believe that a mistake on your side excuses your spouse's adultery. If you place too much emphasis on blaming yourself, you will be absolving your spouse of responsibility. It's also critical that you pay attention to your partner's actions.

2. Avoid Obsessing About The Third Party

If you want to swiftly drive yourself insane, you may ask a million questions about the other guy or woman, spend hours monitoring that person's social media page, or even attempt to

get a sight of this person in person. You may believe that learning everything about this person would help you figure out what went wrong with your relationship, but in fact, this will not provide you with any further answers while causing you a great deal of anguish.
When a spouse has an affair, it is rarely about the third party.

Unless that spouse believes he has begun a genuine connection with a third person, cheating is usually a manifestation of the cheater's discontent with himself or the marriage. If you are too focused on the other guy or woman, you will not be thinking about your spouse or the relationship.

Though knowing certain information about the affair may provide you comfort, you may not want to know too much about the other person's appearance, occupation, or any other characteristics that may distract you or make you feel awful about yourself. It's just not worth it.

3. Don't Attempt To Justify It

Though you may believe that if you can just find a logical explanation for why the cheating occurred, such as the fact that your husband has been feeling powerless since losing his job, or that the third party came on to your wife so strongly that she couldn't possibly resist, it's pointless to try to make sense out of nonsense. Accept that you are upset and that you need to move on, but don't believe that making excuses for your spouse is the way to do so.

What your spouse was thinking when he or she chose to cheat may defy logic. Spend less time attempting to figure out why something occurred and more time focusing on going ahead.

4. Don't Be Concerned About What Your Friend And Family May Think

You may feel wounded and outraged, and you may feel compelled to inform all of your family members, and closest friends, or even post about it on social media to express your sentiments. If you do decide to reconcile and make things work, you will have to deal with others seeing your spouse and your relationship differently for the rest of your life.

Along with keeping what occurred to you private, you should not be concerned about what people who are aware of the affair think. Though others close to you may provide helpful counsel, in the end, it is all about what is best for you. You should not consider what others would think whether you decide to quit or remain in the relationship. At the end of the day, it doesn't matter what everyone else thinks, and you shouldn't allow other people's opinions to influence your decision-making.

Speaking with those close to you may help you acquire strength as well as a fresh perspective on your circumstance. But remember that their views will never replace your own.

5. Do Not Take Large Moves Without First Contemplating

Though you may feel compelled to pack your belongings or push your spouse out of the home the moment you discover the adultery, you should give this more thought. You may undoubtedly spend time apart from your spouse, but avoid declaring divorce or taking dramatic actions immediately. Instead of doing something you may regret later, give yourself time to think about what occurred and what is best for you and your relationship.

Though opting to spend some time apart right away might be beneficial, you should avoid declaring that you want a divorce as soon as you hear the news; although this may be what your intuition tells you to do, wait until you have a clear mind before making a final decision.

6. Avoid Punishing Your Partner

Maryjane

I was so caught up in my grief and fury that I made many errors and hung on to my wrath, and it is only now that I have humbled myself and realized that whatever my husband did not excuse what I did. I accept responsibility for my errors, and I genuinely regret having injured him.

I yearn for him to forgive me; it's heartbreaking to see him suffer and be unable to stop it. As he put it, it's ironic that I created the suffering and now I want to repair it. It took a few months for me to understand I was completely adrift once he discovered the affair, and I had no idea where to go from there. He is poisonous because he feels abandoned by friends and family. I'm still hoping, and in God's love, I feel it's possible to get through it. It's not simple, and his heart has hardened. Why do we inflict such pain on people we care about?

Though it may feel nice to be cruel to your spouse, to take away the things they like, or even to have your affair in response, this kind of conduct will not get you very far in your relationship. You may be wounded, cold to your spouse, and maintain your distance for a time, but you shouldn't intentionally make an effort to make him or her feel worse, otherwise you'll both wind up feeling bad.

Punishing your partner will just increase your resentment and make your relationship seem even worse. It's OK to spend some time away and to be colder and more distant than usual, but being intentionally unkind will not make things better.

Taking Initiative

1. Establish Your Demands

Before you start a talk with your spouse, you should think about what you want from him or her. Don't simply start talking about adultery and then weep and make up. Instead, spend some time developing a game plan so your partner understands what you expect from him if the relationship is to continue. This should not seem like a punishment, but rather like a strategy to go ahead as a group.

Tell your partner what he or she has to do to keep the relationship going. Going to therapy together and potentially separately, taking tangible efforts to rediscover the things you liked to do together, creating time for conversation every night, or sleeping in different rooms until you feel comfortable sharing a place again are all examples.

If you're considering divorce, you should consult with a lawyer as soon as possible. The sooner you accomplish this, the stronger your negotiating position.

2. Give It Some Time

John

I come from a non-emotional background, and I have no clue how to deal with her. Today's most pressing problem is one of trust. She frequently accuses me of things that are false but cannot be proved, namely my thoughts and sentiments. We are no better off after breaking touch with the affair partner for 3 years.

My issue is deciding how to react to the charges. I ended up reacting rather than replying since I have made many changes and am protecting myself. This is certainly not the best approach to handling things, but I don't have any other options. I've been urged to take it, but doing so appears to strengthen her beliefs.

My greatest suggestion is to listen to and validate the accusers' suffering and anxieties. Your wife is trying to get over the agony while also deciding if she can or should trust you again. She wants and needs safety to recover. Assuming she hasn't already slammed the door on ever trusting you again, your unwavering empathy for her agony at not knowing whether she can trust you will ultimately get through.

It will be simpler to decide what to do if you see the charges as an expression of her fear and agony of being deceived again, as well as a scream for your unwavering love and comfort. 3 years may seem like a long time for her to be in so much anguish and terror, but a shattered heart doesn't last long.

Being patient, comforting, and addressing her sorrow and anxiety when she accuses will ultimately disarm her since acknowledging her anguish will improve her trust and diminish the fear impulse. Recognize her anguish and fear while loving her through it. I believe your failure to reply to her has given her the impression that you are uninterested. You must find a method to convey empathy for her anxieties and pain while assuring her of your unwavering loyalty.

Even if you are ready to forgive your spouse or return to normalcy, you should be aware that it might take a long time to restore the trust and love you previously had for your spouse. Even if you're both committed to making it work, it might take a long time for things to seem "normal," for want of a better phrase, and for you to develop feelings for the person you married. This is quite normal. You may get into problems if you attempt to hurry things.

You will not be able to forgive your lover or return to normalcy overnight. It might take months, if not years, to reestablish confidence. You'll also have to take it slowly. It may take several days for you to feel comfortable sleeping in the same bed as your partner, going out to dinner with him, or enjoying the activities you used to enjoy doing together. Be ready for that.

3. Express Your Emotions

Hiding or concealing your emotions may result in a wide range of harmful and bad emotions. Taking the effort to recognize and comprehend the many emotions you are feeling is beneficial to your mental health.

Be ready to convey to your spouse how much you are suffering after a time of caring for and attending to your own heart. Be as open as possible about your emotions of abandonment, worthlessness, betrayal, fear, and uncertainty. You will help maintain the channels of communication open between you and your partner if you share freely and honestly.

Inform your spouse of your feelings. Tell him about your rage, hurt, betrayal, and suffering as a result of his actions. Don't put your guard up and appear as if it wasn't a huge problem; instead, let him see your grief and hear how you're feeling.

You will never be able to fully move ahead together if you are not honest and transparent about what you are going through. Even if you are hesitant or afraid to express your actual sentiments, you must do so.

If you're scared about confronting your spouse or speaking what you want to say, you may write everything down. That way, you won't get caught up in the moment and neglect to convey a crucial point.

If you are too upset to speak about what occurred, wait a few days or until you feel comfortable talking about it as frankly as possible. Of course, the discussion will never be fully comfortable, but you may take your time getting your bearings if necessary. However, you may not want to put off this talk for too long.

4. Ask The Questions To Which You Desire Answers

You may want some clarification on what your unfaithful spouse did. If you want to piece together how this has been going on, you can ask how many times it has occurred, when it occurred, how it began, or even how your spouse feels about this other person. However, if you want the relationship to last, you should think twice before asking about details that you might be better off not knowing.

Ask whatever questions you believe may help you understand where your relationship stands. However, avoid asking inquiries only to satisfy your curiosity; the answers may be too painful.

5. Arrange For Medical Testing

As humiliating as it may seem, you should both be tested as soon as you learn that your partner has cheated on you. You have no idea what illnesses the third person may have had, and you have no way of knowing whether they were passed on to you. Though your partner may argue that it isn't essential, it is what you must do to ensure your safety.

Going through this process can also assist your spouse to realize the significance of his or her behavior. Sleeping with someone else while simultaneously sleeping with you has placed you in danger, and you must recognize this.

Sandra

I just discovered that my closest friend, lover, and love of my life, whom I adore and am in love with, cheated on me. When I grew suspicious after discovering improper text messages or emails, the problem rapidly became my fault for "looking through my things" privacy this and that - I would be the "bad" one for going through and reporting anything!

The problem of infidelity found its way to me through an STD, and God knows I've been loyal from the first time I lay eyes on him! I'm finding it tough, if not impossible, to communicate with my lover. It's all been horrible, and I'm holding onto a thread right now. Please pray for me because this is the most paralyzing anguish that has left me feeling embarrassed, dishonored, less of a lady, in deep deep despair, constant sobbing, and lack of appetite.

I never imagined he would do this, and I am terrified because of all the emotions I am experiencing, but I feel imprisoned by the situation, and most importantly - His response to my knowledge about it, and his overall response to his transgression will ultimately determine if I can survive this horrible event, which I do not wish on Anyone.

I'm also upset that the other lady knows who I am and knows how madly in love I was with this guy - and still decided to go down that road with him. I try hard not to think about the scenario but there are times throughout the day and night when I see an image in my brain that makes me want to weep and curl up in a ball. In fact, for some strange reason - maybe because he is alive and I know he chose to do what he did - I have to say it is the most traumatic incident. And for me, it indicates he was prepared to put our relationship in jeopardy.

I realized I was in love with this guy because I am not willing to jeopardize our relationship. Never, ever, ever in a million years. I hoped he felt the same way about me. So, in the end, I'm not that exceptional after all. The agony is just overpowering, and the last few minutes have been soothing for me. I find myself wanting to appease him, practically letting him dictate how we deal with this circumstance.

6. Pay Attention To Your Partner

Though you may be upset, overwhelmed, deceived, furious, or any number of other feelings, it is critical that you sit and listen to your spouse. You may feel like hearing him or her out is the last thing you want to do, but if you want to take the relationship ahead, you must hear his or her side of the story. You may discover new sentiments or frustrations in your relationship that you were unaware of.

It's not fair to assume he doesn't deserve to share his side of the story or to feel anything in this situation. Though you may not be ready to address your spouse's sentiments, if you want to go ahead, you must allow him to express himself.

7. Every Day, Work To Improve Your Communication Skills

After you and your spouse have begun to discuss adultery, you may focus on strengthening your communication lines. Make an effort to be open and honest, to communicate regularly, and to avoid being passive-aggressive as much as possible. Though it may seem difficult after what your husband did, you must communicate as effectively as possible if you want things to improve.

Once you're ready, make it a point to meet every day, ignoring all distractions, and discussing how your relationship is progressing. If you feel like you're just reliving previous sentiments, you should concentrate on talking about the present and future rather than the past.
You and your partner must communicate about how you're feeling. This is the moment to be extra cautious and focused

on your connection. It's difficult to go ahead if you don't have effective communication.

8. Determine If You Want To Attempt To Remedy It

Of course, once you begin discussing adultery, you must make an essential decision: do you believe you can someday forgive your spouse and have a good relationship again, or do you believe it will never work? It's important, to be honest with yourself and consider if your relationship is worth salvaging. The most essential thing is to give yourself enough time and space to think before making any hasty judgments.

If you've spoken to your spouse, expressed your thoughts, and heard his or her side of the story, and you've had some time to dwell on your sentiments, you may begin to consider if you want to attempt to make things work.

If you decide to make things work, be prepared to put in a lot of work. If you realize your marriage is gone, it's time to file for divorce. If this is the road you want to take, you should research the regulations in your nation and/or state, since they might differ quite a little.

Relationship Reconstruction

1. Always Do What Is Best For You

Unfortunately, no magazine, friend, family member, or doctor can advise you on the best option for you—or your family. If there are children involved, your choice becomes much harder. Though you may believe there is only one correct option, at the end of the day, you must be honest with yourself and listen to what your heart is telling you. It may take some time to discover the truth, but the most essential thing is that you acknowledge that no one else, including your husband, has the authority to tell you what to do or feel.

This might be a frightening concept since you will almost certainly need some time to think out the solution. But if your instinct is already telling you anything, you should pay attention.

2. Make The Decision To Forgive

Remember that forgiveness is a decision; it is not something that occurs or does not happen. If you want to forgive your spouse, or even attempt to forgive him or her, you must make a firm decision to do so. Forgiveness will not simply fall into your or his lap; you must strive for it. Accepting that you'll strive to make things work is the first step.

Tell your spouse the truth about this. Don't allow your desire to forgive or not forgive to go unnoticed. Tell him or her that you are determined to make things work.

Make an effort to forgive your spouse.

Forgiveness will be a journey and a process. It is unlikely to happen fast or easily. Learn what forgiveness is and is not. Choosing to forgive your spouse does not imply that you will suddenly forget the grief and anguish caused by their infidelity. It is, however, more about the health of your own heart. You will want to express your forgiveness to your spouse at some time.

3. Spend Time Together Without Discussing The Affair

If you want to begin repairing your relationship, you and your spouse should spend quality time together that is unrelated to the fact that your partner strayed. Work on doing activities you used to like doing together and avoiding areas that remind you of infidelity. Make an effort to begin from the ground up, ensuring that your connection has a firm foundation via regular activities before moving ahead too quickly.

You could even find a new pastime to pursue together, such as hiking or cooking. This might assist you in seeing your connection differently. Just make sure you don't get the impression that your spouse is hurting or trying too hard.

4. Look For Yourself

When you're coping with a cheating spouse, taking care of yourself may seem like the last thing on your mind. You may be too preoccupied with a tornado of conflicting emotions to consider basics like eating three meals a day, getting some sunlight, and getting enough rest. However, if you want to remain strong during this tough period and have the stamina to focus on your relationship, you must do just that.

Make an effort to obtain at least 6-8 hours of sleep every night. If you can't sleep because your partner is lying next to you, you should feel at ease proposing other sleeping arrangements. Avoid isolating yourself. Spend more time with friends and family to feel more at ease.

5. Seek Professional Help

Though therapy isn't for everyone, you and your husband should give it a go if you're trying to work things out. You may fear that it will be too humiliating or too much for you, but it may be the ideal way for you and your partner to establish a secure atmosphere in which you can genuinely feel comfortable communicating your thoughts.

Find a counselor you can trust and offer your best throughout your sessions. If this is vital to you, make it plain to your husband that you must attend. Your spouse betrayed your confidence, and he or she should be able to help you with this.

6. Ensure Your Children's Safety

Dealing with an unfaithful spouse becomes much more difficult if you have children. Your children will most likely sense the stress in your family, so it's essential to be upfront and honest with them about your and your spouse's troubles.

While you don't have to go into great depth, let them know you love them and that you and your spouse are trying your best to solve the problem.

If you're considering divorce, don't allow your spouse to use your children to shame you into staying. While he or she may claim that having two parents at home is better for your children, this may not be the case if those two parents are always bickering or no longer care for one another.

Make time for them even if you're coping with a difficult scenario. Being with your children might also help you feel stronger.

7. You'll Know When It's Finished

If you've tried everything to make things work and still can't see yourself forgiving your spouse or moving forward, it may be time to call it quits. Don't berate yourself for being unable to forgive your spouse, even if he or she has worked hard to regain your trust; some things simply cannot be forgiven. If you discover that you simply cannot continue the relationship and that you have made every effort to make it work, it is time to make the decision and move on.

Don't be angry or frustrated with yourself if you find it difficult to forgive. You've worked hard, and your partner is the one who betrayed your trust in the first place.
You shouldn't be ashamed of yourself for "giving in" if you've been able to move on. You've made a decision that you

believe is best for your relationship and family, and no one should judge you for it.

Allow yourself time to mourn your loss. You cannot force someone to love or stay with you. Consider whether you truly love him or simply despise rejection. Moving on is difficult. Make sure you're not romanticizing him or the relationship. You deserve to be treated better than this.

CHAPTER 3 : THE 17 MOST COMMON UNFAITHFUL SPOUSE MISTAKES

1. Carrying On With Normal Life

Julie

I recently confirmed my husband's relationship with a woman from another country. They met last year while she was on vacation in Africa. I had my suspicions, but I recently created a Facebook account and discovered evidence of them communicating.

I'm not sure how far they went, but my suspicions were aroused when she sent a thank you card to our house in appreciation for my husband's assistance during the family trip. I questioned him, and he shrugged as if it were nothing. This betrayal has caused me great pain. This man is fantastic. And he claims to love me and wants this marriage to survive, but I'm not sure I can trust him.

He has agreed to see a marriage counselor. I'm in shock and can't think clearly. My initial reaction was to leave, but he asked me to stay and work this out. How will I proceed if I can't trust this man? I don't believe he understands my pain or what I require to begin healing.

You can't go on living your life normally if you want to heal your marriage after a betrayal. Your normalcy is what got you into this mess. Changes must be made to reassure your mate that you are accepting responsibility for your problem and taking proactive steps to prevent it from happening again.

I had clients who go to the bar or stay out late without telling their spouses where they are or who they were with. To some, it may appear simple to ensure and concretely build safety, but it cannot be overstated.

Taking responsibility for your betrayal includes avoiding high-risk situations and obtaining the necessary assistance to return your life and the life of your partner to safety. This is a must if you want to rebuild your marriage. Make them aware of the changes you've made in your life to foster a culture of safety. These are the things that will convince her that this is not life as usual.

2. Attempting To Justify Your Affair Partner

Kelvin

I had a 7-month relationship with my boss. I had fallen in love, or so it seemed and was on the point of abandoning my wife and children. However, my integrity would not allow me to go, so I stopped the affair and informed my wife two weeks later.

My wife and I have been in recovery for three months, both in combined treatment and individually for me. My "detoxification" from the affair has been harsh. I was emotionally attached to my Boss, and we still work at the same company.

It has grown easier during the last three months. While my wife is aware that I was in love with my boss, I have not communicated the full degree of my anguish over the termination of the affair since it is difficult for her to comprehend. I don't protect my boss, but any action that might harm my boss is tough for me. I'd prefer to be free of any emotional relationship with my boss, but I can't wish my feelings away.

My wife and I recently argued over placing images of my wife and me at our office - not because I am opposed, but because my wife saw my concern. I completely understand that my wife wants our marriage to be represented at the workplace, and I do as well. But I can't help but want to avoid hurting my boss. I'm uploading the photos. My inquiry is not about the images of course I should put them up; of course, my wife wants that; of course, it helps send a signal to my boss; of course, my hesitation hurts my wife.

My issue is how to cope with the feelings associated with wanting to protect my Boss. I don't want to feel like this, yet I can't help myself. It's probably part of letting go of the affair, and it's surely a problem of working together. My wife and I are discussing the possibility of quitting my work. But is it normal for me to not want to harm my boss, and how can I overcome this?

It may seem obvious, but don't defend the other woman or man. Your friend will most likely trash the affair partner or, if you've been using porn, she may try to trash you. Do not attempt to defend your affair partner.

It is easier for your spouse to be angry with the affair partner than with you, and if you defend the affair partner, your mate is likely to believe that you are more loyal to the affair partner than to your mate and your marriage.

3. Being On The Defensive

Alice

I am really upset and have not yet decided whether to remain; he has yet to completely realize or freely address the whole issue, with some defensive behavior and avoidance to fully reveal it. It's almost as if he's guarding something holy and doesn't want to lose it by sharing it with me; it's excruciatingly difficult, but I have the heart condition to be patient; we have a family. I've decided to be patient since it took us ten years to get here, and it will take time to recover whatever is salvageable.

I am optimistic and open-minded, and I would advise any injured spouse to have an open mind, especially if children are involved, and to avoid departing the partnership for no other reason. Take the time to determine if it is still worthwhile to save. Making major, life-altering choices while furious and in pain is never a good idea.

We put pressure on ourselves to rush through a resolution, but if it isn't necessary, please be patient with your pace. As I already said, it is too early to tell, but I recognize that individuals make errors and that I own responsibility for the breakdown. Let us all be kind to one another and try to remember what drew us together in the first place. As remote as it may seem now, it may be what keeps us going ahead and healing from our grief.

Taking personal responsibility is the antidote to defensiveness. When speaking with your injured spouse, the most important thing to avoid is becoming defensive. If you get defensive, your partner will believe you don't understand and will proceed to increase the volume.

Examining what transpired is incredibly unpleasant for the unfaithful spouse, but minimizing, blaming one's companion, or even blaming another person is not a solution.

Because the discovery of a betrayal is so devastating, there is no opportunity for defense. You should use two phrases: "You're right" when they are correct and "I deserve that" when they are wrong. Answering "why" questions is difficult at best. Any explanation you provide will be misconstrued as an excuse.

The greatest solution to why questions are to inform your friend that you will do everything possible to find the answer, but that you don't want to come off as defensive while attempting to answer a question you don't know the answer to. Don't be defensive in any way.

You could be thinking at this moment, "I don't want to assume full responsibility; my wife or husband contributed to what occurred. This relationship had problems long before I had an affair." While this is true, the first order of business should be to stabilize the marriage. Allow your partner time to heal before addressing the other concerns in the marriage. One of your first measures will be to avoid becoming defensive while speaking with your friend.

4. Pointing Up Your Friend's Flaws And Failings

Chloe

My hubby defends other women, but continues to bring out my weaknesses as if I didn't already know- he deflects and twists the conversation against me as if I had done something wrong.

I'm not unattractive, and I'm not obese. I'm not sure why he feels the need to disrespect me when all I want is answers. I want to get past this because I love my husband.

There are flaws in every marriage, but now is not the time to address them. First, you must restore the relationship's faithfulness and stability. Then, after the relationship has been healed, you may address additional concerns. Before any concerns inside the betrayed spouse can be handled, the unfaithful spouse must learn to accept the focus being on their own lives early on.

5. Believing that if you and your affair partner do the right thing and return to respective marriages, the affair will end.

In truth, one partner probably valued the connection more than the other. As a result, just because you decide to terminate the affair doesn't guarantee the other person will, or even that you will.

The Break-up and Make-up cycle is a normal component of a relationship. But you can't start healing your marriage unless you take a position and deny all contact. But don't be foolish; the next effort or impulse to connect will arrive. Denial of an oncoming reality will only expose you to relapse. So prepare yourself for the need to politely but firmly decline contact.

6. Information Leakage Over Time

Faith

I've been married to my hubby for three years. We lived together for two years previous to marriage; he is in his fifties and I am in my forties. This is not our first marriage.

I pondered. I discovered it. Someone mature and established. I didn't find out about the affair until after we were married! 3 months later- because the tramp he was dating had provided me screenshots of their messages over the previous several years. Photos that were shared were included. I was enraged!

He said that the romance stopped in December, but we married in April. This lady, on the other hand, leaves vicious notes on my door, telephones me in the middle of the night, and sends me emails. Threats and allegations that they still see each other continue!

I moved back to my house. He apologized profusely. I still love him and chose to work through it. I'm still upset, I'm still asking questions, and I'm still wounded! He advises me to "get over it!" He curses and calls me names. I'm now on watch whenever he interacts with a lady—ecstatic when another woman notices him yes I give him attention and never denied him anything emotionally, intimately.

The disclosure of an affair or sexual addiction is a terrifying process, but one of the biggest errors is attempting to keep the whole truth hidden. Similarly, twisting the facts to make your friend feel better is just as harmful.

The difficulty with leaking information is that it makes it more difficult for your companion to learn to trust you again. If your mate believes you've laid out the whole truth and nothing but the truth, that there are no more surprises or painful revelations to come, and then your mate encounters multiple "oh by the way" or other discoveries as time passes, your mate's ability to believe a single word you say will eventually be destroyed.

As a result, it is essential to set everything out upfront. It's never a smart idea to attempt to dominate your partner via information flow. Your partner will either be able to handle the truth or not. Getting the truth out to your partner, all of it and unvarnished, is a terrific chance to demonstrate true integrity and safety: something you may feel you've lacked if you've had to conceal your acts or lie. Don't pass up this opportunity. As quickly as possible, tell the complete truth.

7. Attempting To Avoid Discussing Your Partner's Emotions

The betrayed cope with the agony produced by infidelity by talking about their emotions. They may need to repeat themselves or ask the same question many times. We are unfaithful and often believe that our deceived friends are bringing it up to make us feel awful or disgrace us. That is not the case; that is just how they recover.

Answer your friend's questions as many times as necessary. They will appreciate your candor in the long run, and you will have helped them recover while also striving to establish a safe' environment for you both to heal.

8. Trusting Anything Your Friend Says

When individuals are upset or emotional, they may say things they don't mean. If your partner says, "I want a divorce," don't automatically assume that you will get divorced. Don't overreact if your friend resorts to name-calling or threatens to kidnap your children. There will always be a lot more talked about than done when everything is said and done. If your friend begs you to go, do so, but don't assume it's for the long term. A new day will almost certainly bring fresh sensations. You can be certain that sentiments will change with time.

Warning: Even if you take your mate's comments with a grain of salt, don't dismiss what he's saying. Listen sympathetically and inform your companion that you heard what was spoken. Just don't base the rest of your life on what a heartbroken spouse says, particularly in the first three months after the affair is revealed. Balance your feelings regarding your friend's words by hearing them truly and knowing that not every word will stay.

9. Taking Your Spouse To The Same Areas You Took Your Affair Partner

Reminders are one of the most difficult challenges that the devastated spouse faces. Taking your mate to a location where your mate is aware you were with your affair partner will cause serious pain to your mate. Be mindful of places that will serve as a reminder and cause pain for your spouse.

10. Deception Of Any Sort

Florence

My spouse was having a romantic relationship with my second cousin. I discovered this by accident. He requested I assist him in recovering his email password. I noticed a lot of texts from her. Messages indicating she wants to be with him. When I questioned him about it, he erased all of the communications.

I also discovered that he attended her birthday party and lied to me about it he said he was at a male friend's party. Nothing was happening, he continued repeating. She even messaged him about me, telling him that I was sly and that he should ask me why I joined social media. Naturally, he denied denied denied. I'm not certain that there was no physical affair.

If my spouse would confess he was wrong and not blame everything on me. I'm sure I could forgive slowly. However, I am furious and do not trust him. I would also respect him more if he would stand up and acknowledge his affair rather than lying about it he lies even when the proof is shown to him. My point is that if you cheat on your spouse, please acknowledge it. Stop being a coward and own up to betraying the marriage.

One of your objectives is to provide your companion with a cause to feel protected. Telling a falsehood, even the slightest one just confirms your mate's opinion that you are untrustworthy. Tell the truth, no matter how tough it may seem. In the long term, your friend will know that you're being honest with them, even if they don't like what you're telling them.

Never Break promises made to your partner. If you tell your friend you're not going out to lunch with another lady, then don't go out to lunch with another woman (or guy, if that's where your temptations lay). If you promise to go to counseling with your husband, then go to therapy together.

If you commit to being home at 5:00, make sure you arrive by that time. If you agree to join an accountability group, attend the meeting. Failure to maintain these sorts of commitments, despite their little seeming consequence, can throw doubt on your whole integrity and make it impossible for your partner to trust you.

11. Failing To Help Your Friend's Rehabilitation

Annabel

I am a 45-year-old highly educated and ambitious woman who has been in a relationship for 16 years, including 12 years of marriage to a man who was a college dropout. We founded a firm together, which he primarily operates successfully, while I work as a medical expert. We have three children. Our relationship was excellent till last year, except that he is unable to disclose his emotions or deeper ideas and is equally unwilling to listen to mine.

He's a very powerful guy, with strong language and sometimes a dictatorial demeanor. But, since I am a demanding wife, we compensated one another in various ways. I'm not attempting to rationalize the situation because I feel it cannot be justified in any manner. However, it is unquestionably the outcome of a deeper issue including emotional desolation.

The last four years have been difficult, particularly for me, since I was dissatisfied with the development opportunities in my sector of expertise, where I felt I was not reaching my full potential. I also had this unsatisfactory sensation of not being able to be myself and freely do things I like without having to consider children, employment, or "permission" from my spouse.

I cheated on him while on a work trip alone which very never occurs with an old friend who is extremely gentle, empathetic, and emotional. The primarily emotional infidelity had been going on for a few months from a far distance, except for two weeks that were not long distance and included a sexual affair. It is about 3 months after D-Day.

My husband first clung to me as if he was afraid to let me go for a few weeks, with loads of amazing sex and vows from his side that we would make it and that he will stand by me. That stage lasted roughly a month. After that, there was a lot of pain, sobbing most of the time for about 3 weeks, and sadness. Following that, there were 3 months of verbal hostility denigration, wrath, accusations, and isolation from stonewalling me, with his theories about how things went wrong.

He's been quieter for a few weeks since he began since my health was badly failing, but not been very helpful to me or the relationship. He continues stonewalling me, stating he's done with it and just remains for the kids, but when I want to file for divorce, he kicks back and urges me to start the process since he's fine in the present scenario.

He may be really harsh and verbally abusive, yet after a few hours, he'll hug me tight and become a little closer positively. He expects me to tell him everything, has access to my phone, email, and everything, and goes insane if I decide to go out while he is gone every night, without informing him where or with whom. He rejects couples counseling, fabricates tales about other women he is meeting and refuses to do anything enjoyable with me. When I tell him that this is not the way to build a relationship and that retribution would not offer him pleasure or fulfillment, I feel that is all he needs.

He claims he has to handle things at his speed and in his manner, and that I can take it or leave it since that is his method of dealing with it. He claims to need space and time, but he is unsure of what he wants or where this will go. He also cannot guarantee me future fidelity. What should I do in this situation? Should I go or stay? And for how long, and what boundaries should be established?

Both spouses are disoriented by the sorrow of discovering a betrayal. Both the husband and wife will battle with how to deal with the event's grief. It might be disheartening at times since the damaged spouse typically takes longer to recover from the initial shock than the unfaithful spouse.

In these cases, the devastated spouse wants to understand what occurred and communicate about it; the unfaithful spouse may often see this as an effort at retribution. This may lead to the unfaithful spouse ceasing to support the other's rehabilitation. It may be tempting to encourage your friend to just get over it at some time.

In reality, although it may seem to be a good idea in terms of moving on if the first phase of recuperation is not allowed to run its course, it might lead to future difficulties. If your companion suppresses her/his sentiments and does not comprehend what has transpired, the sensations will resurface in around 6 years.

In actuality, you are much better off supporting your friend's healing at the time of the betrayal than living with a mate who is suffering and will ultimately blow out for six years.

There is an evident difficulty with trust after a betrayal. An unfaithful spouse must be consistent in what he or she says and does to reestablish confidence. You may believe that a tiny contradiction is insignificant since you know your heart's state and purpose, but your companion does not.

Your actions are the only thing a heartbroken spouse can rebuild on. If you are consistent and do what you say, your companion will begin to trust you again. However, failing to follow through on what you say will simply help to strengthen your mate's skepticism. It is critical that you express what you mean and that you mean what you say.

Don't make the mistake of telling your friend what you believe she or he wants to hear but then failing to follow through. You'll be considerably better off if you're realistic and then follow through on what you say, even if what you say and then follow through on isn't as spectacular as you or your friend had hoped.

12. Asking Your Friend To Forgive You

In general, never ask someone to forgive you. You may inquire, but do not reveal. Your partner will have to struggle through the process of forgiveness. It has nothing to do with you in many aspects; it's a gift your companion must offer herself/himself. If you do not forgive, your friend will stay a victim. It's much preferable to inform your mate that you want her/him to forgive you and to ask if there's anything you can do to assist your mate heal and forgiving or to make the process simpler for them.

Also, don't hit your friend over the head with religious rhetoric, reminding him or her that now that you've requested forgiveness, it must be granted. If you tell your friend to forgive, he will get resentful and find it more difficult to forgive you. Be a part of the solution rather than the issue.

13. Failing To Respond To All Of Your Friend's Queries

This is a difficult one. Personality type best determines how much knowledge a person needs to recover. Some people need minimal information before they can comprehend what has occurred and move on. Others need vast volumes of data before they believe they comprehend what has occurred. For these people, what they don't know hurts them. Usually, their imaginations are considerably worse than reality.

The gift of answers to inquiries is one of the most valuable presents you can offer. Tell your partner you'll answer all of his questions, but if you believe he's asking them out of rage and an effort to damage you, request a time-out. Tell your partner that you'll provide whatever information is required, but you'd want to allow her/him 24 hours to pray or think critically about whether she/he wants that knowledge. Then, at the end of 24 hours, if your friend still wants the answer, offer it to them honestly and totally, without any twisting.

It is critical to provide your mate with the facts she or he believes is required since your mate must rewrite the history of your relationship. It will be difficult, if not impossible, to go on until this assignment is completed. Don't withhold information that your spouse will need to proceed.

14. Ignoring Your Friend

Victoria

My spouse continues telling me that the affair is done and that I should let go and move on. It's been over two years since I made the discovery, and my emotions are like hell. I learned a lot of things on my own at first, then by asking a lot of questions, and many times by fighting and arguing with my spouse.

He keeps stating he wants peace and then walks away. He claims he wants to leave a couple of times after big disagreements! I sometimes feel like doing that, but I have a lot of things to think about, including the kids. He's polite and wants to reconcile, but he can't stand it when I abruptly alter my attitude.

There are many ways to injure your partner, and being passive-aggressive is one of them. It is fairly unusual for the unfaithful spouse to feel upset about what has occurred and how the damaged spouse has reacted in response to the suffering.

Because it may seem wrong for the dishonest spouse to be outraged, and they have no right to be verbally abusive, some unfaithful spouses attempt to harm their companion by refusing to speak. Both aggressive and passive hostility are meant to harm your partner. Both show a lack of affection. Give your partner the gift of communication to aid in his or her healing.

15. Attempting to rally all of your friend's friends and family to your cause

You may be expecting that these may assist your friend in waking up and seeing reality. Some of your pals may join you. But it doesn't imply your friend will listen. In reality, this method is quite likely to backfire and build animosity and resentment against you. If you use this strategy, other friends may believe and support the reality that your husband is proper in leaving someone so domineering.

16. Endangering your friend

At the time, it may seem that your threats would cause your spouse to "see the light" and persuade her/him to "fly straight." However, it is critical to avoid using threats since they create misleading motives for complying with your objectives.

Threats cause anxiety, remorse, and humiliation. While these motivators may help your partner pursue your intended course of action in the near term, they will only be successful as long as these sentiments cause suffering. Your friend will lose motivation as the fear, guilt, and humiliation wear off.

You would be considerably better off being supportive and telling your partner, I hope you choose to remain with me, but I want you to do what God tells you to do. Mate coercion might push your spouse away.

17. Playing chess with your children

This is often done to persuade one's partner to remain. However, this will only harm your children. If your partner is adamant about leaving, pressuring or influencing him or her to remain is neither good nor beneficial for your relationship or family.

CHAPTER 4: WHEN TO WALK AWAY AFTER INFIDELITY: 7 SIGNS IT'S TIME TO GO

Cheating is without a doubt one of the most difficult situations you and your spouse may ever encounter. If your marriage has gone through it, you are all too aware of the fear, fury, and sorrow that may result.

This maelstrom of negative feelings is exacerbated by the fact that it may be difficult to know when to walk away after infidelity.

In reality, in all types of marital betrayals, that's a tough judgment to make. After all, infidelity isn't always obvious as an adulterous affair. Perhaps your spouse engaged in an emotional affair.

Perhaps you've been a victim of financial infidelity. Whatever you're going through, important choices must be taken. Divorce is a frightening concept, yet it is often the only option.

You most likely still love your spouse, but is it enough?

Let's go through seven concrete signals that you could be better off leaving a cheater than sticking it out.

Most common reasons to leave after infidelity if your partner has cheated on you, these are seven symptoms that it's time to end the relationship:

1. Your Partner Refuses To Apologize

Glory

I discovered his infidelity over a year ago. Last year, I attempted to keep my sorrow and disappointment hidden. It worked for most of the last year till today. I'm furious at myself, at him, and love in general. I weep a lot. I'd want him to chat with me. He closes me out and avoids it, as well as gaslights. It's gotten to the point where I feel like my love for him is fading. He has not been there to help me achieve closure.

I've been left to sort out the answers for myself, which are horrifying. To digest knowledge, I am the sort of person that needs a lot of questions answered. He's gone completely off the deep end with that. It just hurts, and I'm sick of feeling hated.

If your partner betrays you in this manner but refuses to show regret, they are effectively informing you that the marriage is gone.

Even if they don't believe cheating is a serious relationship sin, they should care enough about your emotions to apologize.

Words are free, and if they can't get the courage to apologize, you have no reason to assume that your relationship will improve in the future.

It's becoming clear that your spouse isn't such a decent person, and you should leave before they injure you again.

2. Your Spouse Refuses To Attend Counseling

Josh

I've delayed far too long to start doing the appropriate thing for my rehabilitation. My partner refuses to communicate with me. I want her to know I'm serious about this. I've committed to the practice of not focusing only on healing at all times. My greatest errors are failing to follow through on my promises and becoming defensive (the biggest problem).

Marriage counseling is the single most effective way to save your relationship. If your spouse refuses to try it, you're in for a serious issue.

It's vital to remember that cheaters shun couples counseling for reasons other than disinterest. Many individuals (particularly guys) are uncomfortable talking about their emotions, but it may also get quite confusing.

For example, if your cheating spouse is devout and feels that infidelity is against God's word, they may assume that seeing a therapist is unnecessary before reconciling with God. That's why you may have to do some digging to figure out what's wrong.

If you've gotten to the bottom of it and your unfaithful spouse still won't budge, your chances of surviving this difficult period are slim.

I recommend you get expert support for yourself at that time to prevent some of the most common errors made by freshly separated persons.

3. Your Partner Does Not Demonstrate A Desire To Work

Maybe your spouse agrees to go to therapy with you, but you can tell they're merely saying it for show. Even the finest therapist cannot assist a marriage in recovering from adultery if both sides are unwilling to open up.

If you've been trapped with a spouse who has been going through the motions after their affair was revealed, it's time to get unstuck.

4. They Are Still In Contact With The Person With Whom They Cheated On You

James

I recently had a romantic affair that ended in disaster. My wife discovered the truth, forgave me, and wants to work on our marriage. I feel like there's no chance for our marriage; I can't even let go of this love affair partner, and she won't talk to me since I'm married. How can I move on and on when I feel my heart belongs to the lady with whom I had an affair?

This is the definition of adding insult to injury. Your spouse admits to having an affair, claims it's ended, and then believes their (allegedly) former lover is a good buddy.

Rosa

He told her we weren't together because we were divorcing. He informed her that we were in the process of divorcing. It's been two years, and I still believe he was happier with her. He met her family and friends and even vacationed with her on many occasions. He had the chance since he pretended to be so busy with work.

How can someone who claims to love me do this? He stated he had to play a part with her because he was weary of her, but it seems to me that you kept it continuing for a purpose. She handed me a text message in which he said nice things to her, such as "I miss you" and "I've never felt this way before." It crushed my heart since we have children. He was with her for two years, and throughout that time, he not only placed me in a corner but also our children.

Even if the affair is finished, this conduct displays a profound disregard for you and your emotions, and you should not tolerate it. This affair has traumatized you, and you shouldn't have to be reminded of it all the time.

Calling it quits with your spouse because they keep in touch with the individual with whom they cheated on you does not make you envious; it keeps you sane.

5. Your Partner Doesn't Appear To Be Dedicated To The Relationship

Freeda

However, since she is his supervisor, he was unable to discontinue any communication with her.

And the reason I didn't trust him was his stubborn determination to obtain another job and cut all links with her.

I found him sending her improper text messages and Facebook private messages again not more than a year later. She then promoted him and assigned him to work long, late hours alongside her.

Then she sent him out on her errands while pretending to be at work. Of course, when he accepted the promotion, I went completely insane. Every late night ended in an allegation and a brawl. And there was the little hussy at work telling him that his home life was interfering with his ability to perform his job and that he needed to get his mind straight regarding his home life.

Then he began pushing... going out, staying out all night, making obvious falsehoods, playing mind games with me... it all blew out on February 10. He was residing in her residence by February 15, and the same day he says he moved in with her, he withdrew me from the bank account where his salary was placed.

He declares that he is finished. He wants to divorce. He despises me and cannot tolerate me. I'm suffering from too much anxiety. Is that a justification to have an affair and divorce?

Finally, he informed me that he took it because he knew it would end the marriage and that his marriage had already ended a year before he met her, there you have it... the 'workaround' reason for never having done the 'work' to heal from the affair in the first place.

Since their infidelity became public, your spouse may have been open to all of your recommendations for how to restore your marriage, but they haven't come up with any of their own.

Someone who wants to sort things out should seem excited and involved in the healing process; just going along with it isn't enough. Things will not work if your spouse does not seem to be fully dedicated to making things work.

If you're carrying all of the relationship weight, it's time to let go and find someone who believes you're worth the effort.

6. They Constantly Lie

Vicky

I apprehended my husband of 23 years but he denied everything. I feel for a purpose since I was headed into our bedroom to inform him I'm leaving because of his affair, but largely because he refuses to acknowledge any of it when caught red-handed. I'll be back on in the morning since I don't have any privacy while he's here. I'm getting to the point where I can't bear going to bed...This man was my whole world but he betrayed me.

Jane

My spouse has a history of pouring information on me. Just when I thought I was getting over it, he sugarcoated everything and lied to me. All of the information was false. Now that it's been a month, I'm finding it tough to cling on, and why should I be hanging on to a liar?

Jackson

I discovered about two weeks ago that my wife, the one person I believed would never lie to me, had been having an affair for years with the one man she knew I couldn't tolerate. She's always been a flirt, as am I, but I've made it obvious that I despise this man.

I never imagined she would have time since we work together and are practically always together. I discovered out by mistake when we were away from home, but when I challenged her, she denied it, saying it was just talk and nothing serious.

She spent most of our vacation time texting him and sending him videos/photos. After hours of prodding, she revealed they had been together once, but it had been years; nevertheless, days later, after further prodding, I discovered it was still happening on, with their last time together being last summer, but the messages continuing until two weeks ago.

She claims that despite the texts stating that they will meet when she returned home, that she missed him more than he missed her, that it was not going to happen. She maintains she has no affection for him, yet in the chats, she said that specific clothes were solely for him.

I'm convinced she has affection for him, but she denies it. If she is lying about caring for him, I believe she is also lying about caring for me. She has broken off touch with him, not concealing her phone from me, but I'm curious if she has another identity for him that allows them to communicate.

One minute I want to repair our marriage, the next I'm not sure I can, and I'm not sure I'll ever be able to trust her. We're still away from home, terrified of what will happen when we return. I love her, but I can't forgive her or trust her, and without those things, what's the sense in attempting to salvage our marriage?

We've all heard the phrase "once a cheater, always a cheater" when a married guy cheats on his wife.

In reality, that isn't always the case, but if your marriage has a history of dishonesty and deception, you're unlikely to ever be able to trust your spouse, and it's time to spare yourself the heartache.

This is true even if your spouse no longer seems to be lying about anything significant. After an affair has undermined your trust, even tiny falsehoods may be very upsetting because they remind you of the betrayal you experienced.

This gives you no chance to reestablish trust and go forward together. That is why recurrent dishonesty may be grounds for divorcing and starting over with someone else.

7. The Cheater Refuses To Accept Responsibility And Instead Places Blame On Others

Cheating does not appear anywhere. We're all products of our upbringing, and we all can act out when we're unhappy.

However, if your partner uses other people to explain cheating, your relationship may not be worth salvaging.

This is especially heinous if you are the one your spouse blames for their adultery. They put you through one of the most terrible experiences of your life, and now they're blaming you?

If that's the message you're getting, your spouse is treating you with a degree of antagonism that makes reconciliation impossible.

However, regardless of who is to blame, this might be a deal breaker. If your spouse claims that it wasn't their fault that they cheated, they're saying there's nothing they can do to avoid it from occurring again.

You'll never get the piece of mind you need to go on with your life until they accept responsibility.

Now that you've considered if your relationship can or should withstand infidelity, let's look at some facts. The combined knowledge of individuals who have been in your shoes before might guide probable next moves.

Perhaps you'll even see how you and your spouse fit into the greater picture.

CHAPTER 5 : HOW TO EXPRESS YOUR LOVE TO YOUR SPOUSE AFTER AN AFFAIR

Though errors happen in partnerships all the time, affairs are among the most difficult to reconcile. You have now made the fatal error of cheating on your spouse. You've violated your partner's trust, and you're now wondering how to mend your relationship. Let it be acknowledged that repairing your marriage will be a difficult task.

It will take a lot of effort to confront someone who previously trusted in you but now recognizes your flaws. It will require considerably more work to reestablish your spouse's trust in the relationship.

So, how can you express your love for your spouse after an affair?

Your responsibilities from now on
You have several vital responsibilities as an unfaithful spouse. Your spouse will be devastated as a result of the betrayal. Perhaps they got symptoms of PTSD.

What you must do to assist them in working past the first shock is as follows:

If you haven't already, put an end to the affair. Be truthful with your lover and show regret for what you have done. Work through your partner's feelings alongside them. Promise not to make the same errors again—and to learn from them.

Melissa

It's been two years since he confessed on D-Day. We had been married for 10 years and had suffered many losses. I was the youngest daughter of an alcoholic mother and an abusive father, and he was the only kid reared by an abusive mother. To say the least, my spouse and I came into the marriage with a lot of baggage.

My husband maintained touch with the lady for almost four months after the affair. He persisted in his dishonesty and refused to be open. I was too traumatized at the moment to leave him. It took him three years before he began to participate in honest behavior, but it has left me unable to build trust and has created an even bigger personal barrier between us.

We went through what is known as hysterical bonding immediately after the affair, which implies we were actively engaged in our intimacies. However, after I was free of the trauma, a massive internal barrier formed. We seemed to be chatting, having passionate sex, or fighting like cats and dogs.

Finally, enough transpired for my husband to wake up and begin working on the relationship; but, his tales changed so often that it was difficult to know what the reality was. Now, I believe he is telling the truth, and he is a lot better spouse than he was before, but I can't seem to get over my mistrust.

This is what occurs to the betrayed party when the betrayer fails to perform his or her duties. Dishonesty, whether by omission or outright falsehoods and conflicting accounts, will wreak havoc on the relationship.

If you have betrayed your marriage and want to remain married to your spouse, the only way to go through that journey and gain trust is to engage in healing talks with honesty, love, and empathy, otherwise, your marriage will suffer from the actions of mistrust that occur afterward.

Transparency and honesty are required to demonstrate your love for your partner. Checking in with your spouse, giving them any text messages or emails you have received, and often telling them you are sorry and love them are all instances of this.

You should also consider if you have provided adequate information concerning the situation. In most circumstances, nothing will satisfy your partner or provide them with adequate closure as complete transparency. Tell them everything that occurred, including why it happened.

Connecting With Your Partner Following An Affair

So you've got a lot of work ahead of you. You must not only be responsible for your acts, but you must also express yourself honestly and give up some of your privacy. Not only that, but you must make an effort every day to show your spouse how much you love them.

Communicate

Talking to your spouse is the finest approach to expressing your love for them. Use the affair to create space for conversation and to discuss the state of your marriage. Consider involving a competent therapist if you are uncomfortable speaking to one another or don't know how. In therapy, the two of you may feel free to express yourself.

It is best to use this time in therapy to work through the issues that led you to cheat on your loved one. This way, you'll both be aware of what you can improve to make your new relationship stronger than the last.

Words Are Louder Than Actions
You have already demonstrated to your spouse that you are serious about maintaining your marriage by admitting your mistakes and ending the affair. You must also support your actions. You and your spouse once had a lot to talk about—you married, after all. However, what you did erase all of that.

You must now outperform yourself. Do what you say you'll do, and you'll be on your way to rebuilding trust between the two of you. Doing chores around the house when you say you will or spending quality time with your partner are two examples.

Patience Is Essential

You may believe that therapy and increased communication will help your spouse get over the affair faster. That, however, is not the case. Everyone handles such emotional trauma in their unique way. Even if you are doing everything correctly, your spouse may lose patience with you. On days when you are already frustrated, you may have to deal with difficult conversations. Maintain your patience. Approach everything with empathy.

Maintain Consistency

It might take months or years to recover from adultery. You should not diminish your attempts to demonstrate affection during this period. Maintain an open and honest communication channel. If there was a previous cycle of blame, do not repeat it. Avoid being impatient or dwelling on the past. You are establishing a new connection, and for it to be successful, you must continually collaborate.

Moving Forward With Compassion

Overcoming infidelity as the cheater is difficult, particularly if your spouse has become distant. It will take time to demonstrate that you love your spouse and want to mend your marriage. You'll have to learn how to speak with one another and work together to solve problems. Such things may seem hard to do alone, which is why you seek the help of a couples therapist.

CHAPTER 6 : 7 WAYS TO PREVENT INFIDELITY IN YOUR MARRIAGE

Marriage is the highest act of commitment that two people can make to one other, pledging that they will stay together through good and bad times, illness and health, and everything else that life may throw at them until death do them part. There's only so much a married couple can do to prepare for life's unexpected curveballs, but there are strategies to safeguard your marriage against infidelity.

This is not to say that if you do these things to defend your marriage against adultery, no one will ever go astray, but by fortifying the fortress, you make it a bit more difficult for anyone else to breach the castle!

Preventing infidelity in marriage is also not something that can be accomplished by just one partner. It's a team effort, just like the rest of the marriage. So gather your team and go through the following measures to defend your marriage against infidelity with them.

Every individual and every relationship must define what infidelity means to them. Is it merely a physical connection, or is it also an emotional one? Where do you draw the line between being close friends and maybe endangering your relationship? Do you have any reservations about having close friends of a certain gender around your significant other?

Have an honest and open talk with your spouse about your present level of comfort with what seems dangerous to your relationship and what doesn't. No one should feel as if they are not permitted to have close friends because their spouse feels threatened by them, and no one should feel as if their partner is unconcerned about their emotions. Dial into both of your thoughts on what constitutes marital infidelity and reach a mutual understanding of what is and is not cheating in your marriage.

ESTABLISH BOUNDARIES

Consider limits to be the road map to a happy marriage; if you want to know where you're going, follow the map! Laying out your expectations for your marriage makes it much simpler for you both to live up to them since you can't blame someone for not meeting your standards if you never informed them what they were. Marriage boundaries may strengthen your relationship.

What kind of texting/social media connection is permitted?

What privacy expectations do you have for your phones and social media?

Marriage does not necessarily imply that your spouse has unrestricted access to your phone and social media accounts, but there should be nothing on there that makes your spouse feel uncomfortable in the relationship, which may be a difficult line to tread based on your unique privacy expectations. Everyone has the right to have friendships outside the marriage, and everyone has the right to feel secure inside the marriage.

You might specify settings such as notifying one another when you are privately texting someone of the opposite sex or the same, depending on your orientation or notifying one another when there will be a rendezvous. This kind of agreement allows your spouse the courtesy of knowing when you're in a potentially troublesome scenario.

In reality, most concern about things like private messages or business lunches happens because the spouse involved made no mention of them; feeling as if things are being concealed makes it seem as if there is anything to hide, even if there isn't.

Setting specific boundaries around communication and connection with others will also serve as an internal alarm for you both: if you're feeling uneasy about disclosing a lunch date to your partner, you might want to dig a little deeper to figure out where that's coming from; is this "just a lunch date" to you, or are you experiencing other emotions as well? It might serve as a reference point for you in terms of how you see your interactions with others.

KEEP IN CONNECTION

There's a lot to be said about keeping a connection in a relationship, but the most crucial aspect is to consciously come together with your partner. It is all too easy to realize that in the hustle and bustle of everyday life, we have pushed deliberate time spent together to the back burner. Yes, you may still have breakfast and supper together every day, but are you making an effort to be there and connect?

One of the most effective strategies to safeguard your marriage against infidelity is to ensure that both of you are engaging in the relationship, which takes time and effort. Putting each other at the top of your To-Do lists should emphasize time spent together going on dates, spice things up, or even visiting a counselor together if you're caught in a rut you can't seem to break out of. People who commit to a relationship are significantly less likely to cheat on their spouse.

GROWING UP TOGETHER

One of the most effective strategies to make your marriage cheat-proof is to guarantee that you and your spouse develop together rather than apart. This includes not just spending the time to connect as indicated above but also ensuring that you and your partner continue to have new and interesting experiences together. It is normal and natural for people to develop new interests as they progress through life, and having individual interests is good and healthy for couples, but you also need to have shared interests!

Look for things you and your partner can do together to strengthen your bonds, such as taking dance lessons, learning a new language, creating and crossing things off. Make sure that whatever you choose is something that both of you want to do, since resentfully participating in an activity will not enhance your marriage.

TOGETHER TRAVEL

What better way to make new, exciting memories and cement your team's status than to travel together? There's a whole world out there to discover; whether you're looking for romantic getaways in the United States or romantic getaways around the world, there's no shortage of fantastically romantic destinations for you and your partner to visit!

Travel is not only healthy and enjoyable for you both individually, but traveling as a couple allows you to remember that you are a team, doing life together. Couples that travel together also tend to have better sex lives! When searching for measures to defend your marriage against infidelity, make sure you and your partner are enjoying wonderful, adventurous adventures together to remind you both why you don't need anyone else.

TALK ABOUT YOURSELF

One of the greatest methods to maintain your marriage affair-proof is to continue communicating your feelings to each other. It's easy to think that your spouse understands how much they mean to you or how much you enjoy being married to them, but it never hurts to remind them. Determine your and your spouse's love languages (most individuals have two) and utilize them to your advantage if you don't already know. If your partner's words of affirmation and acts of service are words of affirmation and acts of service, you may need to amp up the way you demonstrate your love via words and service!

If you want to keep your marriage safe from infidelity, you and your spouse should constantly seek methods to make each other feel valued in the relationship. You may accomplish this through presents, gestures, date nights, or words, but the main thing is to never assume that your spouse understands how much you value them. If you both feel valued and respected in your relationship, it is less likely that either of you will seek affirmation elsewhere.

RELATIONSHIP CHECK-INS SHOULD BE REGULAR

At this point, it is evident that the best method to safeguard your marriage against infidelity is to nourish and build the relationship from the inside, and to do so, you must first identify the weak points! Regular relationship check-ins enable you and your partner to be open and honest about what you both believe needs greater attention.

What exactly is a relationship check-in? It may be as simple or as complicated as you and your spouse decide, but as long as you and your partner check in with each other on how you are both feeling in the relationship, it matters! Make it a delightful date night by preparing your favorite appetizers, popping a bottle of your favorite wine, and then discussing how you both are feeling in your marriage.

Having frequent relationship check-ins is one of the most significant strategies to affair-proof your marriage since it means you and your spouse will be able to tackle anything that arises in the marriage before it becomes a serious problem.

When it comes down to it, there are numerous ways to protect your marriage from cheating, but it's important to remember that we cannot control each other. Even the most beautiful marriages have misunderstandings and miscommunications that can lead to one person doing things that hurt the other and damage the relationship's trust, and that's just human nature.

The honest answer is that you cannot prevent your spouse from cheating. When someone cheats in a relationship, the only one who should be held accountable is the cheater. However, if you follow the advice above for how to safeguard your marriage against infidelity, you'll discover that you've done all you can to improve your connection and reduce the probability of cheating in your marriage, which is always excellent for the health of your relationship.

CHAPTER 7 : Surviving Infidelity: The Top 20 Things You And Your Partner Must Do

The unfaithful spouse must accomplish the following things for your marriage to survive:

1. He must be completely truthful with you about everything. He must honestly and completely answer all of your questions. He must reassure you that asking inquiries is acceptable—within limits.

2. He must do everything possible to convince you that you are the one he wants to be with. He must demonstrate his affection for you. He must be nice, patient, empathetic, and understanding.

3. He must understand your anguish, comprehend the misery he has caused you, and must bear complete accountability for his conduct.

4. He must discontinue all communication with the affair partner and refrain from attempting to protect them.

5. He must convince you that doing what is required to heal will not push him away. He must identify and soothe you when you are suffering or having an affair trigger.

6. He must be able to express and demonstrate his regret.

7. He must reassure you that you are not to blame.

8. He must set aside his own emotions of guilt and humiliation to assist him in recovering.

9. He must reconnect with you emotionally, psychologically, and physically and remain connected.

10. He needs to concentrate on restoring trust. There are no secrets. There is no privacy.

11. He must be eager to seek professional help.

12. He must understand what is and is not appropriate while interacting with people of the opposing gender. He must establish and not cross limits.

The following are the actions that the deceived spouse must take:

1. Allow him the time he needs to demonstrate his love and devotion to you.

2. Be honest about your emotions.

3. Ask yourself the key questions.

4. Don't worry about driving him away while you're trying to mend.

5. Stop holding yourself accountable for his behavior. You have no responsibility.

6. You must be able to connect with him. This will take some time.

7. You must continue to monitor him for him to regain trust.

8. You must be willing to seek therapy to avoid being locked in a stage of recoveries such as anger or despair.

The idea is that for a marriage to survive infidelity, both couples must abandon their inhibitions and hang-ups and work hard to make it happen.

CHAPTER 8 : CONCLUSION

For couples who want to rebuild their relationship on a new foundation, It takes time and patience to rebuild. Just as a tornado-damaged house can often be rebuilt to be stronger and more enduring than it was before, so can an affair-damaged relationship.

It necessitates that the individuals involved commit wholeheartedly to doing whatever it takes to rebuild trust, love, and intimacy between them. Similar to building a house, there is a lot of debris that must be cleaned up and sorted through before construction can begin. It is frequently necessary to seek outside advice. It is not a process to be taken lightly, and professional assistance is required.

The good news is that as a marriage counselor I have discovered that couples who choose to recover from and rebuild their relationships after infidelity often end up with stronger, more loving, and mutually understanding relationships than they had before.

There is still hope, no matter what difficulties you and your spouse face or how deep your pain is. God can mend broken hearts and restore what has been lost. Thousands of marriages with complex and painful situations like yours have been transformed with the help of caring professionals who understand where you are right now.

www.ingramcontent.com/pod-product-compliance
Lightning Source LLC
LaVergne TN
LVHW050338160826
845677LV00014B/3669